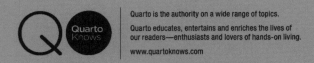

First published in the UK in 2017 by Wide Eyed Editions,
an imprint of The Quarto Group,
The Old Brewery, 6 Blundell Street, London N7 9BH, UK QuartoKnows.com
Visit our blogs at QuartoKids.com

Important: there are age restrictions for most blogging and social media sites and in many
countries parental consent is also required. Always ask permission from your parents. Website
information is correct at time of going to press. However, the publishers cannot accept liability for
any information or links found on any Internet sites, including third-party websites.

One Hundred Things to Spot copyright © Quarto Publishing Plc 2017
Illustrations by Naomi Wilkinson 2017

A catalogue record for this book is available from the British Library.

ISBN 978-1-78603-032-0

Illustrated digitally

Set in Fugue, Bebas Neue and Futura

Published by Rachel Williams
Designed by Karissa Santos
Edited by Katy Flint
Production by Dawn Cameron

Printed in China

1 3 5 7 9 8 6 4 2

MIX
Paper from
responsible sources
FSC® C104723
FSC
www.fsc.org

ONE HUNDRED
THINGS TO SPOT

WIDE EYED EDITIONS

HOW TO USE THIS BOOK

In this book there are one hundred things to spot. They are hidden in different places. Can you find them all?

COLOURS IN THE JUNGLE

A white moth

An orange orang-utan

A blue bird

A grey bushbaby

A purple bug

A cat

A multicoloured chameleon

And a little brown mouse!

1. SEE AND SAY EACH OBJECT.

2. TURN THE PAGE TO LOOK FOR THEM.

3. SHOUT AS YOU FIND EACH ONE.

An orange orang-utan!

WHICH COLOURS CAN YOU SPOT HERE?

4. CAN YOU FIND THE CAT AND MOUSE?

One bear

Two foxes

Three owls

Four
rabbits

Five

squirrels

A cat

And a little mouse!

HOW MANY ANIMALS CAN YOU SPOT HERE?

COUNTING IN SPACE

Six rockets

Seven moons

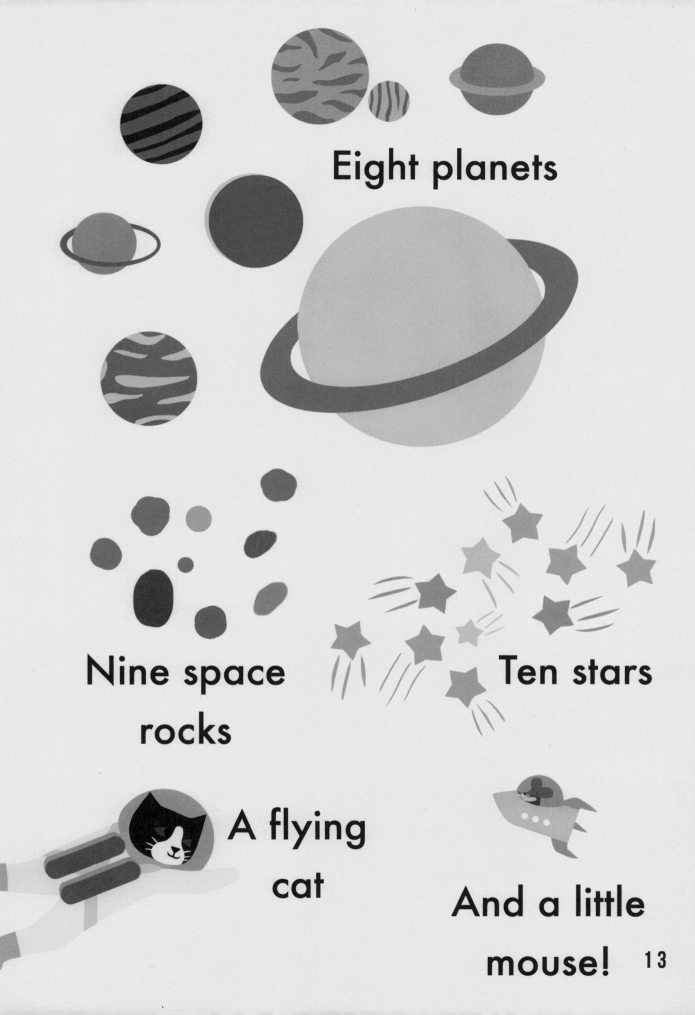

Eight planets

Nine space rocks

Ten stars

A flying cat

And a little mouse! 13

HOW MANY THINGS CAN YOU COUNT HERE?

COLOURFUL THINGS IN THE GARDEN

A black and white cat

A black bird

A red ladybird

A green
frog

A yellow bee

A blue butterfly

A pink worm

And a little
brown mouse!

WHICH COLOURFUL THINGS CAN YOU SPOT HERE?

19

A hot kettle

A sweet strawberry

A cold fridge

A salty pretzel

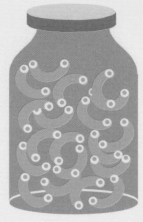

A full jar

An empty jar

A big cat

And a little mouse!

WHICH OPPOSITES CAN YOU SPOT HERE?

SHAPES AT THE BEACH

A starfish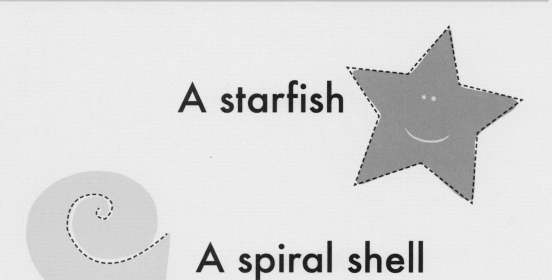

 A spiral shell

A rectangular beach towel

 A triangular ice cream cone

A round ring

A square sandcastle

A cat

And a little mouse!

WHICH DIFFERENT SHAPES CAN YOU SPOT HERE?

27

THINGS AT THE CAFE

A bag under a table

A chair behind a table

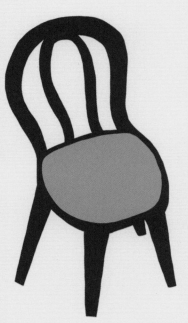

Sugar next to a cup

A cookie on a plate

A waiter in
front of a
blackboard

A parasol
above
a table

A cat

And a little mouse!

WHICH THINGS CAN YOU SPOT HERE?

CAFÉ

30

OPPOSITES IN THE BATHROOM

A dry dog

A wet dog

Some light bubbles

A heavy washing basket

An open cupboard

A closed cupboard

A cat

And a little mouse!

WHICH OPPOSITES CAN YOU FIND HERE?

SIZES AT THE FAIRGROUND

A small ticket

A big bear

A short queue

A long queue

A tall
woman

A short boy

Thick stripes

A cat

Thin
stripes

And a
little mouse!

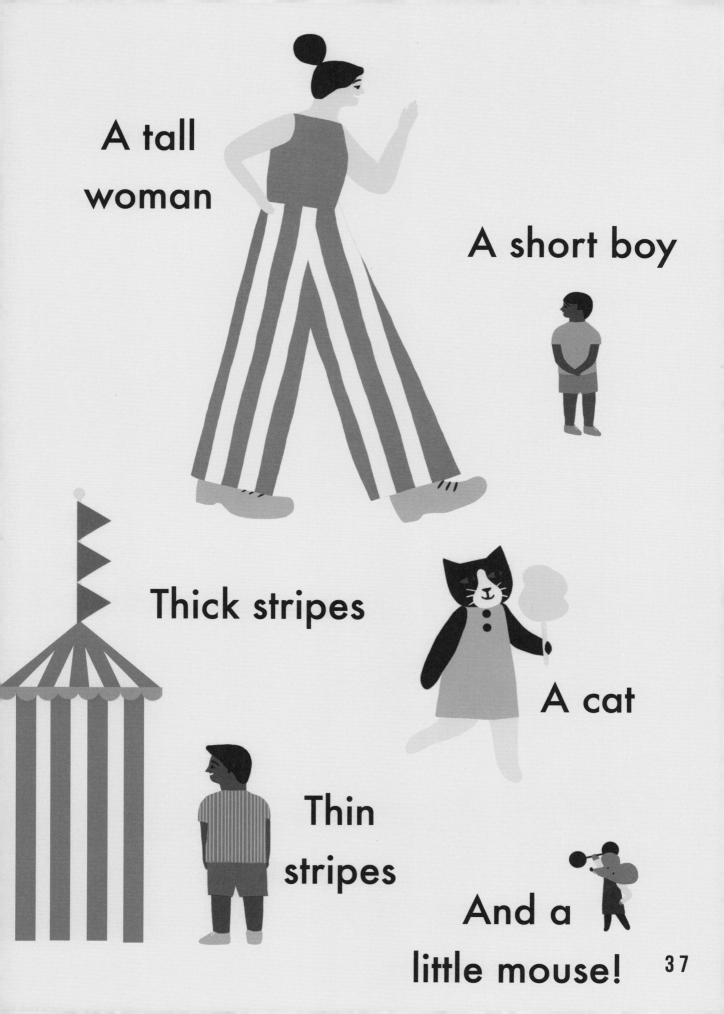

WHICH SIZES CAN YOU FIND HERE?

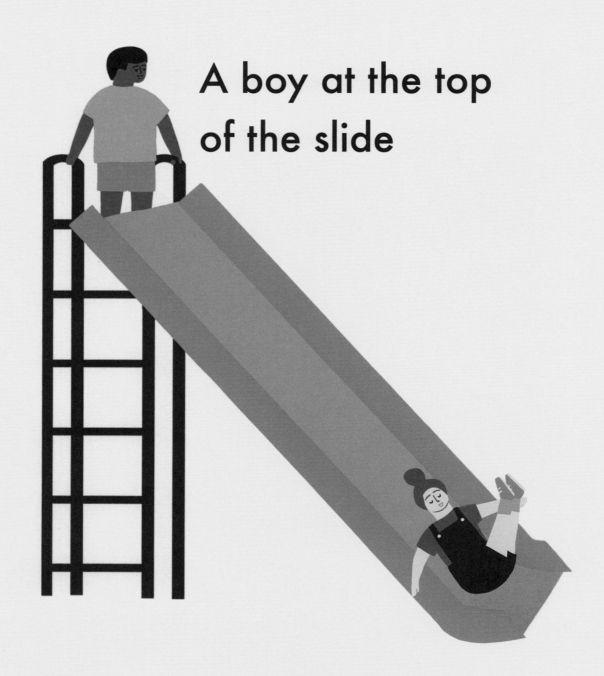

A boy at the top
of the slide

A girl at the
bottom of the slide

A slow snail

A fast bike

A bird on a high branch

A cat

A little mouse on a low branch!

WHICH OPPOSITES CAN YOU SPOT HERE?

A hard diving board

A soft robe

A fluffy dog

A bumpy slide

A sticky lolly

A furry cat

And a little mouse!

WHICH TEXTURES CAN YOU SPOT HERE?

A sad boy

A happy girl

A surprised girl

A shy child

An embarrassed
boy

An angry
chef

An excited cat

And a hungry
little mouse!

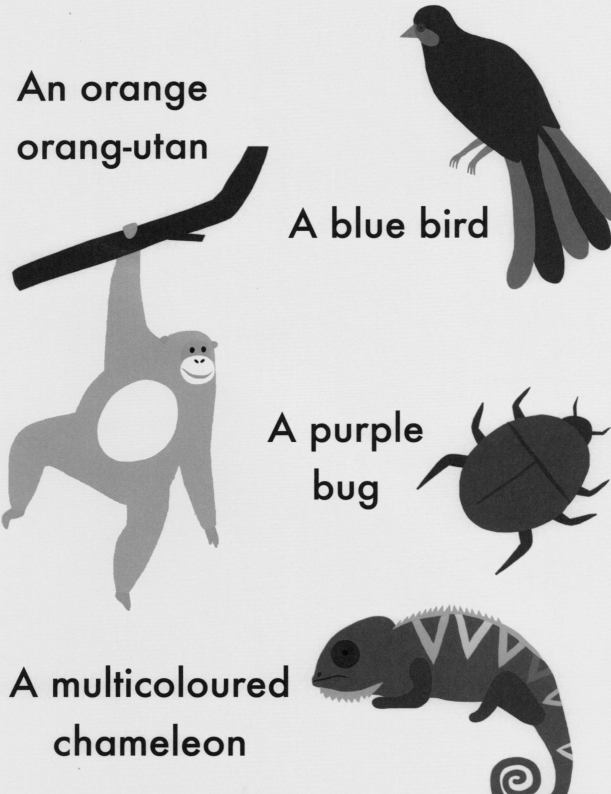

An orange
orang-utan

A blue bird

A purple
bug

A multicoloured
chameleon

52

A white moth

A grey
bushbaby

A cat

And a little
mouse!

WHICH COLOURS CAN YOU SPOT HERE?

54

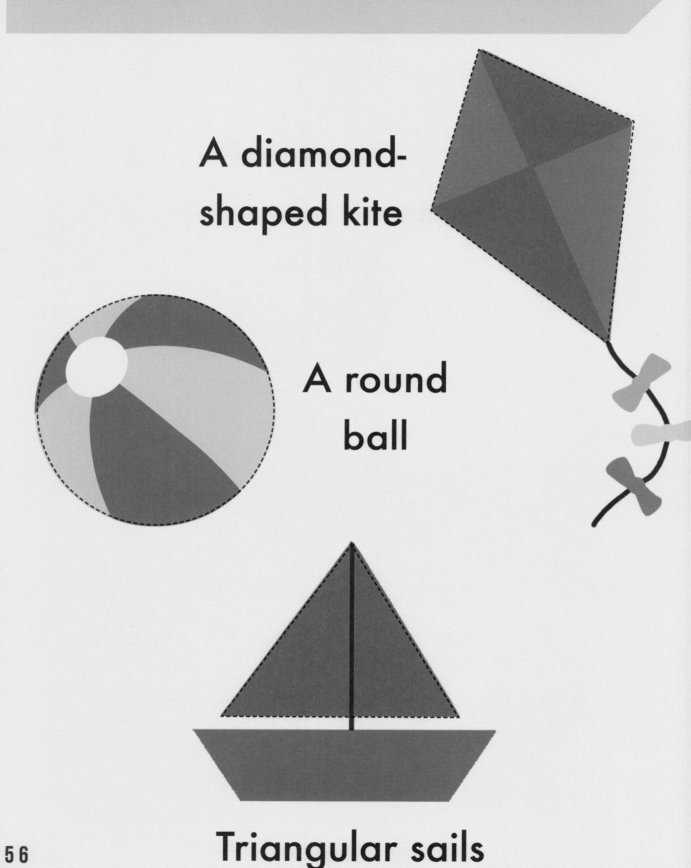

A diamond-shaped kite

A round ball

Triangular sails

Rectangular blocks

A cat with a square bag

A little mouse with a heart lolly!

WHICH SHAPES CAN YOU SPOT HERE?

A camouflaged
zookeeper

A zig-zag
snake

A stripy
tiger

 A butterfly with
wavy wings

A speckled
egg

A spotted
leopard

A cat

 And a little mouse!

WHICH PATTERNS CAN YOU SPOT HERE?

One triangular tent

A cat

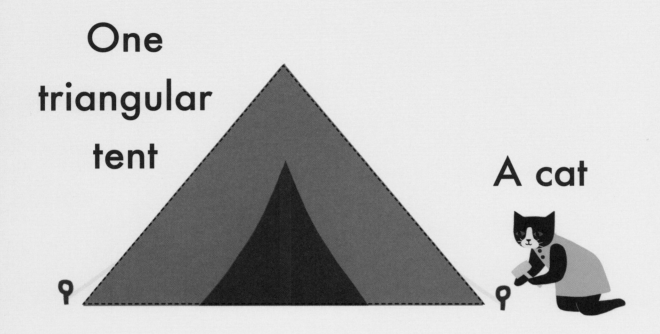

Two rectangular backpacks

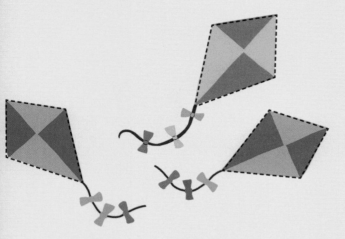

Three diamond-shaped kites

Four square lamps

And a little mouse!

Five circular trees

HOW MANY SHAPES CAN YOU COUNT HERE?

Six green turtles

Seven pink jellyfish

Eight yellow fish

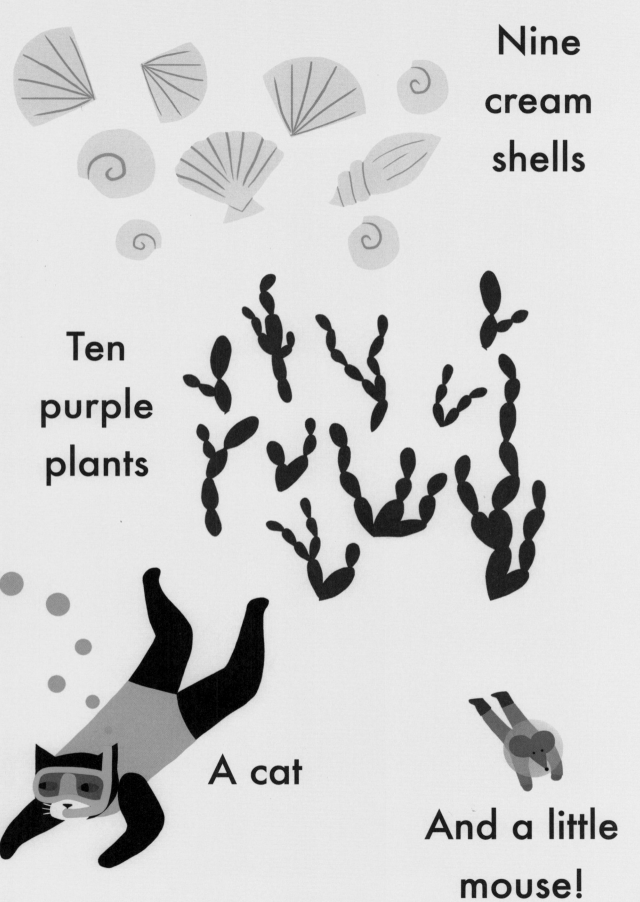

Nine
cream
shells

Ten
purple
plants

A cat

And a little
mouse!

69

HOW MANY COLOURS CAN YOU COUNT HERE?

A bright moon

A dark sky

An awake cat

A shelf above
the bed

A sleeping girl

Roller skates
below the bed

And a little mouse!

WHICH OPPOSITES CAN YOU SPOT HERE?

HAVE YOU SPOTTED ALL ONE HUNDRED THINGS? WHICH ONE HAVEN'T YOU SEEN BEFORE?

ADMIT ONE

Answer: the blue whale